Creating with Fimo® Acrylic Clay

Written by Libby Nicholson
and Yvonne Lau
Illustrated by Tracy Walker

KIDS CAN PRESS LTD.

TORONTO

To my two wonderful children, Christie and Russell,
whom I love with all my heart — LN

To Astrid, my sister and friend — YL

Kids Can Press Ltd. acknowledges with appreciation
the assistance of the Canada Council and the Ontario Arts
Council in the production of this book.

Canadian Cataloguing in Publication Data

Nicholson, Libby
   Creating with Fimo® acrylic clay

(Kids Can crafts)
ISBN 1-55074-310-4 (bound)
ISBN 1-55074-274-4 (pbk.)

1. Jewelry making — Juvenile literature.
2. Modeling — Juvenile literature.
I. Lau, Yvonne. II. Walker, Tracy. III. Title. IV. Series.
TT921.N53 1995   j745.594'2   C95-931694-9

Text copyright © 1996 by Libby Nicholson
and Yvonne Lau
Illustrations copyright © 1996 by Tracy Walker

Kids Can Press Ltd.
29 Birch Avenue
Toronto, Ontario, Canada
M4V 1E2

Edited by Elizabeth MacLeod
Designed by Karen Powers
Printed and bound in Hong Kong

96 0 9 8 7 6 5 4 3 2 1
PA96 0 9 8 7 6 5 4 3 2 1

IMPORTANT

When using Fimo® or other comparable acrylic clay
products, always be sure to follow the instructions
appearing on the product's package, particularly as they
relate to cooking. Small children should always be
supervised. Kids Can Press Ltd. disclaims any liability
which may arise from any use of such products, including,
without limitation, any harm caused by swallowing or the
inhalation of fumes. Neither the Publisher nor the Author
shall be liable for any damage which may be caused or
sustained as a result of the conduct of any of the activities
in this book without specifically following instructions,
conducting the activities without proper supervision, or
ignoring the cautions contained in the book.

Fimo®, Mix Quick® and Pulver® are registered trademarks
of Eberhardt Faber GmbH, a German company.

Kids Can Press Ltd. has published this book independently
without the participation, association, sponsorship or
express or implied endorsement by Eberhardt Faber GmbH.
Kids Can Press Ltd. has chosen Fimo® mouldable materials
as a result of their quality and suitability to the projects
described in this work.

Contents

Introduction

I grew up in Antigua, West Indies, where I spent most of my time on the beaches collecting shells and seaweed, or snorkelling around the coral reefs looking at the beautiful tropical fish. We would often go sailing between the other islands of the Caribbean and see whales and porpoises. The blazing colours of the tropical flowers also inspired me. Even going to the local market with my mother to buy mangoes, papayas and pineapples was an adventure. I couldn't help wondering, wouldn't this all be fun to wear?

I needed to find a material that would let me recreate the colours and shapes that inspired me. In the beginning, I tried working with silver, ceramics and papier mâché, but what I really wanted was a medium with lots of bright colours and a smooth, soft texture that would let me work in three dimensions. Fimo® acrylic clay has all of these qualities.

Once I started working with acrylic clay, I found myself re-creating coral shells, reef fish, rainforest parrots, tropical flowers, market fruit and much more. My childhood dreams of wearing nature had finally come true.

I hope this book will not only encourage you to make beautiful jewellery but will also help you discover your own creativity and experience the magic of colour.

— *Libby Nicholson*

You can make your jewellery any colours you like. If you want to use the same colours that you see in the photos, use the colours listed at the beginning of each set of instructions. The colours that have a number with them, such as #7 caramel, refer to the numbers and names on packages of Fimo® clay.

The other colours are ones you can mix yourself using Fimo® clay colours. Here's a list of our colours and how to make them. To make sun yellow, for instance, take a piece of #15 golden yellow clay, add twice as much #0 white clay, and knead them together until they are completely mixed.

Sun yellow
2 parts #0 white
1 part #15 golden yellow

Tangerine
2 parts #0 white
4 parts #1 yellow
1 part #2 red
2 parts #4 orange
1 part #29 carmine (red)

Light tangerine
24 parts #0 white
8 parts #1 yellow
12 parts #4 orange
1 part #29 carmine (red)

Light pink
4 parts #0 white
1 part #21 magenta

Medium pink
2 parts #0 white
1 part #21 magenta

Dark pink
1 part #0 white
1 part #21 magenta

Skin tone
10 parts #0 white
1 part #4 orange
1 part #21 magenta

Emerald green
1 part #0 white
2 parts #5 green
1 part #37 blue

Turquoise green
1 part #0 white
2 parts #38 turquoise

Light green
1 part #1 yellow
1 part #5 green
1 part #7 caramel

Aqua green
3 parts #0 white
2 parts #5 green
1 part #37 blue

Parrot green
3 parts #0 white
1 part #34 navy blue
3 parts #56 dark olive

Parrot blue
1 part #0 white
1 part #6 violet
1 part #34 navy blue

Periwinkle blue
6 parts #0 white
2 parts #6 violet
1 part #34 navy blue

Turquoise blue
1 part #0 white
1 part #32 light turquoise

Light purple
12 parts #0 white
10 parts #6 violet
1 part #37 blue

Medium purple
6 parts #0 white
10 parts #6 violet
1 part #37 blue

Dark purple
3 parts #0 white
20 parts #6 violet
3 parts #37 blue

Tips

WORKING WITH ACRYLIC CLAY

• Squeeze and knead the clay in your hands to warm and soften it. You can also roll the clay into a long, thin line, fold it several times and roll it again until it is soft.

• To mix colours, roll each colour of clay into a long, thin log. Twist the logs together into one log, fold the log in half and twist it again. Repeat the process until the colours are mixed.

• If your clay is dry and crumbly, add #01 transparent clay to help soften it. One part transparent to four parts coloured clay works best. Transparent doesn't change the colour of the clay. You can also use Mix Quick® according to the package directions.

• To roll your clay into a flat sheet, soften it first. Be sure to use a rolling pin and surface that can't be stained by the clay — ask an adult first. A clean, smooth surface such as a glass table, kitchen counter or any flat plastic surface works well.

• Put any leftover clay in plastic wrap and store it away from direct sunlight and heat.

MAKING BEADS

Use a small marble-size piece of clay for each bead and roll it into a smooth ball. Push a knitting needle halfway through one side of the ball, then remove the needle and push the needle through the other side of the ball to make a hole in the centre. While the ball is still on the needle, shape it as round as possible with your fingers. To remove the needle, hold the bead in one hand and twist the needle out with the other.

AMOUNTS OF CLAY

You can make your jewellery any size you like. To make it the size shown in the photo of each craft, use the amounts of clay suggested in each "You'll need" list.
Here are the sizes:

dot *pea size* *small marble size* *large marble size* *Ping-Pong ball size*

MAKING NECKLACE LOOPS

Roll a small marble-size piece of clay into a log 6 cm (2¼ in.) long and 0.5 cm (¼ in.) in diameter. Shape the ends into points, then fold and press the two pointed ends together to make a loop. Press the joined ends to the centre of the back of the design. Make sure that the loop is big enough for two pieces of cord to fit through.

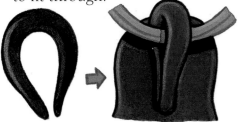

MAKING CORD TOPS

• You can use any cord you like. We use satin cord because it comes in so many colours. Decide how long you want your necklace to be, then cut a piece of cord twice that length.
• Flatten a small marble-size clay ball with your fingers into a long, thin strip about 8 cm (3⅛ in.) long, and 1.5 cm (⅝ in.) wide. Form a loop with the cord and wrap the strip of clay around the loose ends to join them. Smooth the clay into a ball around the ends of the cord and bake together.

STRINGING YOUR NECKLACES

String your baked designs and beads according to the photos in the book or however you like. Make a knot near the end of the cord to form a loop for the cord top to fit through. Centre the clay pieces on the cord and tie a knot just beyond the beads at each end to keep the pieces from sliding.

BAKING

IMPORTANT!
BAKE YOUR JEWELLERY ACCORDING TO THE DIRECTIONS ON YOUR PACKAGES OF CLAY.
• Cover your baking tray with aluminum foil.
• Oven temperatures vary. If your jewellery is shiny after it has cooled, your oven is too hot. If your jewellery breaks, your oven is not hot enough.
• You can use crumpled aluminum foil to prop up the clay pieces while they are baking to keep them three-dimensional.

ATTACHING JEWELLERY FINDINGS

• We find two-part epoxy glue works best, but you can use Goop or any other adhesive made to stick to plastic.
• Make sure you glue earring posts, clips and pin backs to flat areas.
• If you are making dangling earrings, attach the jump rings to the ear wires with needlenose pliers.

Chapter One

COOKIE CUTTING

All the jewellery in this chapter is cut out using cookie cutters. Try the ideas here, then use other cookie cutters to make your own unique jewellery.

Star earrings

YOU WILL NEED

CLAY
#29 carmine (red)
(one Ping-Pong-ball-size piece)

---

small star-shaped cookie cutter

four 7-mm jump rings

two ear wires (shepherd hooks)

rolling pin, kitchen knife, yarn needle,

baking tray, needlenose pliers

1 Using the rolling pin, roll out the clay into a sheet 0.3 cm (⅛ in.) thick. Cut out two stars with the cookie cutter, then smooth the stars' edges.

2 Using the needle, poke a small hole through one of the points of each star to attach the jump rings.

3 Place the stars on the baking tray and bake them according to the directions on the packages of clay. When the stars are cool, use the pliers to attach jump rings and an ear wire to each one.

OTHER IDEAS

Cut shapes out of clay using whatever cookie cutters you like. Mix and match different colours and shapes to make earrings, pins, necklaces and other jewellery. You can use jump rings to hang one cut-out from another, mix in Pulver® for a metallic look, or add texture to the clay for a different look.

Gingerbread man necklace

YOU WILL NEED

CLAY

#7 caramel *(one large and four small marble-size pieces)*

#0 white *(one small marble-size piece)*

emerald green
(one pea-size and two small marble-size pieces)

#29 carmine (red)
(three dots and two small marble-size pieces)

---

small gingerbread man cookie cutter

125 cm (50 in.) light brown satin cord

4-mm knitting needle

rolling pin, kitchen knife, baking tray

1 Using the rolling pin, roll out the large marble-size piece of caramel clay into a sheet 0.3 cm (⅛ in.) thick. Cut out one gingerbread man with the cookie cutter, then smooth the figure's edges.

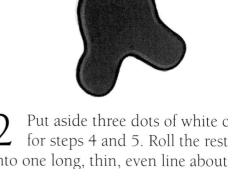

2 Put aside three dots of white clay for steps 4 and 5. Roll the rest into one long, thin, even line about 15 cm (6 in.) long. Lay the line around the gingerbread man. Gently press the line onto the figure.

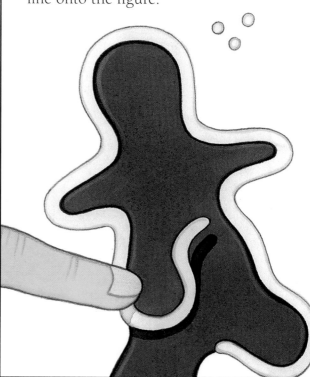

3 To make buttons, roll three dots of the green clay and flatten them slightly between your fingers. Place the three green dots in a row down the middle of the gingerbread man. Make three smaller dots of red clay and place them on the green dots.

4 To make eyes, follow the directions in step 3, but make white dots with green centres.

5 To make the mouth, roll out the remaining dot of white clay into a small, thin line. Place it on the face, as shown.

6 To make a necklace loop, use one marble-size piece of caramel clay and follow the instructions on page 7.

7 To make beads, see page 6. You should make two beads each of caramel, red and green clay.

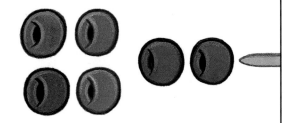

8 To make the cord top, use the last marble-size piece of caramel clay and see page 7.

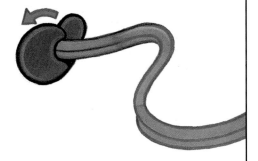

9 Place the pieces on the baking tray and bake them according to the directions on the packages of clay. When the pieces are cool, see page 7 for tips on how to string a necklace.

Christmas tree pin

1 Using the rolling pin, roll out the green clay into a sheet 0.3 cm (⅛ in.) thick. Cut out a tree with the cookie cutter, then smooth its edges.

2 Put aside one-quarter of the red clay for step 4. Roll the rest into a thin line and lay it on the tree for garlands as shown.

3 Roll five dots each of the yellow clay and the pink clay and press them on the tree.

4 To make a candy cane, roll one thin red line and one thin white line of clay and twist them together. Cut a piece about 2 cm (¾ in.) long and bend the top as shown. Place it on the tree.

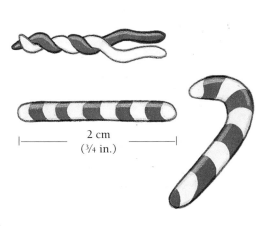

2 cm
(¾ in.)

5 For the star, shape the yellow clay into a disc about 2 cm (¾ in.) in diameter and 0.3 cm (⅛ in.) thick. With the knife, cut five wedges from the clay as shown. Smooth the edges of the star and place it at the top of the tree.

6 Place the Christmas tree on the baking tray and bake it according to the directions on the packages of clay. When the tree is cool, glue the brooch pin to its back.

Strawberry earrings

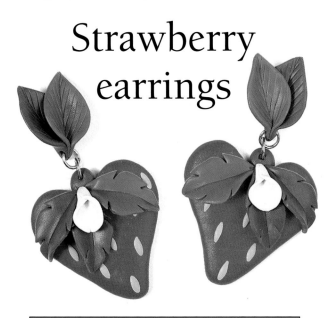

CLAY

#29 carmine (red)
(one Ping-Pong-ball-size piece)

sun yellow *(one pea-size piece)*

emerald green
(one large marble-size piece)

light green *(one small marble-size piece)*

#0 white *(two pea-size pieces)*

---

small heart-shaped cookie cutter

four 7-mm jump rings

two 7-mm earring posts and ear clutches
or two 15-mm earring clips

rolling pin, kitchen knife, yarn needle,

baking tray, two-part epoxy glue

1 Using the rolling pin, roll out the red clay into a sheet 0.3 cm (1/8 in.) thick. Cut out two hearts with the cookie cutter.

2 Smooth the hearts' edges. Round the tips of the hearts so they look like strawberries.

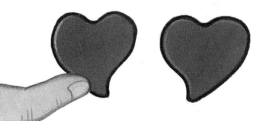

3 To make the seeds, roll the yellow clay into a thin even line and cut sixteen dots. Roll each dot into thin pointed seeds, and press about eight seeds on each strawberry.

4 To make the stems, roll a small piece of the emerald green clay into a little log. Cut it in half and attach one piece to the back of the top of each strawberry. Using the needle, make a hole in each stem to attach the jump rings.

5 To make the leaves, roll the emerald green clay and the light green clay into two logs, each 1.5 cm (⅝ in.) in diameter. Cut six discs of the emerald green, and four discs of the light green, each 0.3 cm (⅛ in.) thick. Shape each disc into a rounded diamond. With the knife, draw a line down the centre of each leaf.

6 On four of the emerald green leaves and two of the light green leaves, cut two little slits on each side of the leaves. Bend the leaves inward along the centre line. Press the leaves to the top of the strawberries as shown.

7 To make the flowers, flatten each piece of white clay into a round disc, curl one side of a disc towards the centre, then curl the other side over the first side. Repeat with the other disc. Press each flower gently onto each strawberry in the centre of the leaves.

8 Using the remaining leaves, make the pads for the earring posts. Draw lines on the leaves as shown, then bend the leaves inward along the centre line. Slightly overlap one light green leaf over an emerald green leaf and pinch the bottoms together. Make a small hole through the leaves for a jump ring. Repeat with the remaining leaves.

9 Place the pieces on the baking tray and bake them according to the directions on the packages of clay. When the pieces are cool, use the pliers to attach the jump rings and join each strawberry to a leaf pad. Glue an earring post or clip to the back of the top of each leaf pad.

Chapter Two

STENCIL CUTTING

Make a pattern, cut your clay, add details and you've got more great jewellery. In this chapter, you'll find out how easy it is to use stencils to make earrings, barrettes, necklaces and more.

Watermelon Earrings

YOU WILL NEED

CLAY
dark pink *(one large marble-size piece)*
aqua green *(one small marble-size piece)*
emerald green *(one small marble-size piece)*
#71 bronze *(one pea-size piece)*

two 7-mm earring posts and ear clutches
or two 15-mm earring clips
white paper
scissors, pencil, rolling pin, kitchen knife,
baking tray, two-part epoxy glue

1 Trace or photocopy the circle stencil and cut it out.

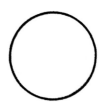

2 Using the rolling pin, roll out the pink clay into a sheet about 0.3 cm (⅛ in.) thick.

3 Place the stencil on the pink clay and cut around it with the knife.

4 Roll the aqua clay and the emerald clay into two lines, each about 12.5 cm (5 in.) long. The emerald line should be a little thicker than the aqua line.

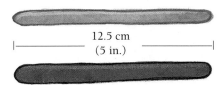

12.5 cm
(5 in.)

5 Wrap the aqua line around the pink circle, then wrap the emerald line around the aqua.

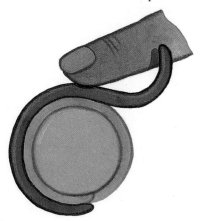

6 Press down on the clay with the palm of your hand to press the pieces of clay together but be sure to still keep the circle shape. Cut the circle in half, then smooth the edges of both pieces. With the knife, draw five lines across the pink, as shown.

7 To make the seeds, roll the bronze clay into a thin, even line and cut eight pieces. Roll each piece to make it thinner and pointed, and press four seeds on each watermelon half. All seeds should point towards the centre.

8 Place the watermelons on the baking tray and bake them according to the directions on the packages of clay. When the watermelons are cool, glue an earring post or clip to the back of each one.

Elephant earrings

YOU WILL NEED

CLAY

turquoise green
(one Ping-Pong-ball-size piece)

medium purple
(one Ping-Pong-ball-size piece)

---

white paper

four 7-mm jump rings

two ear wires (shepherd hooks)

4-mm knitting needle

rolling pin, kitchen knife, scissors, pencil,

yarn needle, baking tray, needlenose pliers

1 Trace or photocopy the elephant and circle stencils and cut them out.

2 Using the rolling pin, roll out the purple clay and the green clay each into two sheets, each about 0.3 cm (⅛ in.) thick.

3 Place the elephant and circle stencils on the purple clay and cut around them with the knife. Flip the elephant stencil over, lay it and the circle stencil on the green clay, and cut around them. Smooth the edges of all the pieces, then set the circles aside.

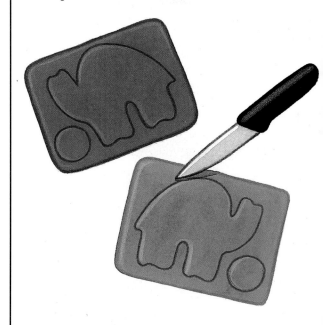

4 To make the tusks, take a piece of green clay and purple clay, each the size of a pea. Roll each piece into a pointed log. Curve the logs, then place the green on the purple elephant and the purple on the green elephant, as shown.

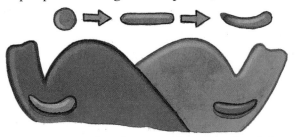

5 To make the ears, form each of the circles into a flat oval. Attach the purple ear over the tusk of the purple elephant and the green ear over the tusk of the green elephant. Press down gently on the front of the ear and lift the back so that it looks three-dimensional.

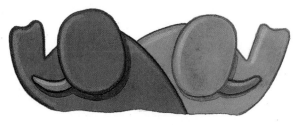

6 To make the eyes, use a small ball each of purple clay and green clay. Flatten each one into an eye base about 0.5 cm (¼ in.) in diameter. Place the purple eye base on the green elephant so that it overlaps the ear. Do the same with the green eye base on the purple elephant. For the eye centres, press a large dot of green clay and purple clay onto the bases, as shown.

7 To make the tails, shape a small piece of the purple clay and the green clay as shown, and place the purple tail on the green elephant and the green tail on the purple elephant.

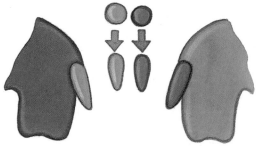

8 With the knife, draw lines on the tails as shown. Draw a line down the centre of the legs on each elephant. Make short lines on each foot for the toes, and lines on each trunk where it bends. Use the knitting needle to lift and curve the trunk. With the yarn needle, put a hole behind each elephant's ear for a jump ring.

9 Place the pieces on the baking tray and bake them according to the directions on the packages of clay. When the pieces are cool, use the pliers to attach jump rings and an ear wire to each elephant.

Animal stencils

It's easy to make fun and great-looking animal jewellery. Follow these directions, then read about each animal for more tips.

1   Photocopy or trace the animal you want to make. Cut around the animal shape to make a stencil.

2   Using a rolling pin, flatten the clay until it is 0.3 cm (⅛ in.) thick.

3   Lay the stencil on the clay and cut around it with a kitchen knife. Smooth the edges.

4   Add the details you see here or decorate your jewellery however you like. If you're making a necklace, attach a loop and make matching beads and cord tops (see pages 6 and 7).

5   Bake your jewellery according to the directions on the packages of clay. Glue on a pin or barrette, or string the animal and beads on the cord.

OCTOPUS NECKLACE

CLAY YOU WILL NEED

dark pink
(one Ping-Pong-ball-size piece)

sun yellow
(one small marble-size piece)

turquoise green *(one pea-size piece)*

(you will need more clay to make the beads, cord top and necklace loop — see pages 6 and 7)

To make spots on the octopus, cut the yellow clay into dots. Roll each one into a ball, flatten slightly and place it on the arms of the octopus. Make two green dots for the eyes and one green line for the mouth and place them on the head as shown.

ALLIGATOR BARRETTE

CLAY YOU WILL NEED
#29 carmine (red)
(one Ping-Pong-ball-size piece)

turquoise green *(one small marble-size piece)*

sun yellow *(one small marble-size piece)*

To make the scales on the alligator's back, cut and shape triangles out of green clay and place them on the alligator. The nostrils are small dots of green clay pressed onto slightly larger yellow dots. Make two yellow dots for the eyes and twelve yellow dots for the toes. Cut two more little green triangles for the teeth.

To make the alligator fit well on the hair clip, press your design onto the barrette and bake them together. You'll still need to glue them together but the clay will be the right shape.

DINOSAUR PIN

CLAY YOU WILL NEED
aqua green
(one Ping-Pong-ball-size piece)

#29 carmine (red)
(one pea-size piece)

medium purple *(one small marble-size piece)*

To make the eye, press a dot of red clay onto the dinosaur's head. Roll eleven small lines, one for the mouth and ten for the claws. To decorate the dinosaur, cut the purple clay into dots and roll each one into a ball. Place the dots wherever you like on the dinosaur.

Chapter Three

MARBLING

By marbling, or slightly blending,
colours together you can make
flowers, birds and fish. Creating
candy canes or striped ribbons is
fun and easy too, once you know
how to marble.

Candy cane earrings

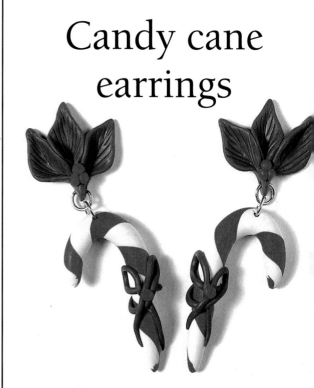

YOU WILL NEED

CLAY

#29 carmine (red)
(one large marble-size and
one pea-size piece)

#0 white *(one large marble-size piece)*

emerald green
(one large marble-size and
two pea-size pieces)

two 7-mm earring posts and ear clutches
or two 15-mm earring clips

four 7-mm jump rings

kitchen knife, yarn needle, baking tray,

two-part epoxy glue

1 Roll the red and white marble-size pieces of clay into two logs, each about 0.5 cm (¼ in.) in diameter. Lay them side by side and twist them together. Roll the log until it is about 10 cm (4 in.) long and cut it into two pieces. Shape the ends of each log into points and bend the logs into candy cane shapes.

4 To make the leaf pads, roll the remaining green clay into a 0.5-cm (¼-in.) diameter log and cut it into six pieces. Shape each piece into a rounded diamond. With the knife, draw lines on each leaf, as shown. Pinch the bottom of the leaves and bend them inward along the centre line.

2 To make the bows, roll the pea-size piece of green clay into a thin, even line. Cut two pieces, each 7.5 cm (3 in.) long. Wrap one piece around a candy cane and make two loops to create a bow, as shown. Repeat for the second earring. Using part of the remaining piece of red clay, place a dot on the centre of each bow.

5 Join three of the leaves at the bottom and make a hole across the base with the needle. Repeat with the three remaining leaves. Make six little red balls for berries. Place three berries on each group of leaves.

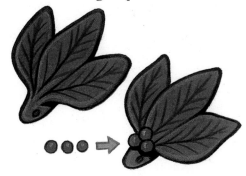

7.5 cm (3 in.)

3 With the needle, make a hole close to the top edge of each candy cane for the jump rings.

6 Place the pieces on the baking tray and bake them according to the directions on the packages of clay. When the pieces are cool, use the pliers to attach the jump rings and join each candy cane to a leaf pad. Glue an earring post or clip to the back of each leaf pad.

Angelfish necklace

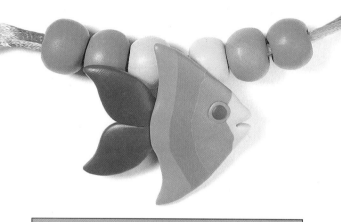

1 Set aside a small ball of blue clay and a dot of purple clay. Roll a small marble-sized piece of each colour of clay into a log 0.5 cm (¼ in.) in diameter and 5 cm (2 in.) long. Arrange the logs as shown. Set the purple log aside for the tail.

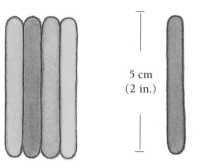

5 cm
(2 in.)

2 Cut a triangle out of the logs, as shown, with the yellow at the top and the blue at the base.

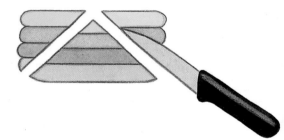

3 With the palm of your hand, press down on the triangle to join the colours together. Shape the triangle into an angelfish, as shown.

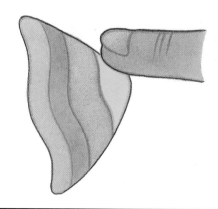

4 To make the tail, shape the ends of the purple log into points. Fold the log into a **V** and pinch the middle together to make the tail base. Shape the tail as shown and flatten each side. Place the tail under the middle of the blue clay and press both pieces firmly together.

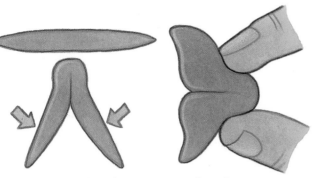

5 To make the eye, use the clay you set aside in step one. Roll a small blue disc for the eye base and a purple dot for the centre. Place them as shown on the pink strip. Cut a little slit in the yellow for the mouth. To make the fish three-dimensional, put the fish face-down in the palm of your hand and gently press down in the centre.

6 To make a necklace loop for the fish, use blue clay and see page 7.

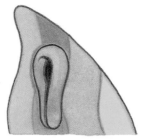

7 To make beads, see page 6. You should make two beads each of the yellow, pink and green clay.

8 To make the cord top, use pink clay and see page 7.

9 Place the clay pieces on the baking tray and bake them according to the directions on the packages of clay. After they are cool, see page 7 for tips on how to string a necklace.

OTHER IDEAS

Make a starfish and a seashell (see page 40), add loops to them and string them on your fish necklace.

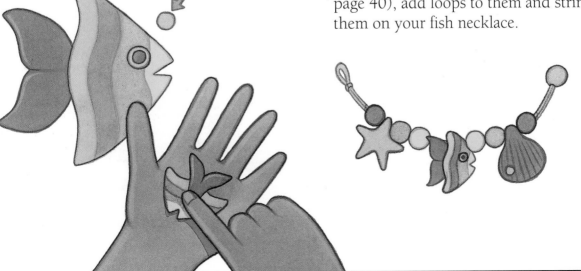

Striped-bow button covers

1 Using the rolling pin, roll out each colour of clay into a sheet about 0.3 cm (¹/₈ in.) thick.

2 With the knife, cut two white rectangles and three red rectangles, each 4 cm x 5 cm (1 ½ in. x 2 in.).

5 cm (2 in.)

3 Neatly lay one rectangle on top of the other, beginning and ending with the red. Trim the edges so that they are even.

4 Cut down through the clay, as shown, to make ten strips. Eight of the strips are for the bow loops and tails, and the remaining two are for the centre bands on the bows.

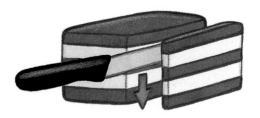

5 Lay the strips down flat and flatten them into rectangles measuring about 6 cm x 1.2 cm (2¼ in. x ½ in.).

6 To make the tails, fold four of the strips into upside-down V's, as shown. With the knife, cut a triangle out of each of the ends.

7 To make the loops, pinch the ends of the other four strips into points. Loop the ends into the centre as shown.

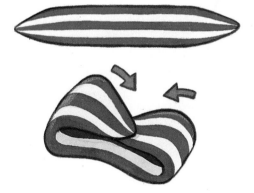

8 To make the centre bands, cut the remaining strips down the middle of the centre red strip. Cut four pieces each 1.5 cm (⅝ in.) long. (Use the remaining clay for another project.) Wrap each band around the centre of each loop. Place the loops on the tails, as shown, and press them together.

9 Place the bows on the baking tray and bake them according to the directions on the packages of clay. When the bows are cool, glue a button cover to the back of each one.

TIP

If the bows don't cover the button covers, cut circles of red clay that are the same size as the button covers. Smooth the edges and place a bow on each one. Bake, then glue to the top of each button cover.

Camellia earrings

YOU WILL NEED

CLAY

medium purple (*one Ping-Pong-ball-size piece*)

turquoise blue (*one Ping-Pong-ball-size piece*)

---

thimble

two 7-mm earring posts and ear clutches
or two 15-mm earring clips

rolling pin, kitchen knife,

two-part epoxy glue

1 Using the rolling pin, roll out both balls of clay into sheets about 0.3 cm (⅛ in.) thick.

2 Use the thimble to cut out six circles each from the purple clay and the blue clay. Cut all the circles in half and join a purple half with a blue half. Smooth the edges of the circles and flatten them into ovals.

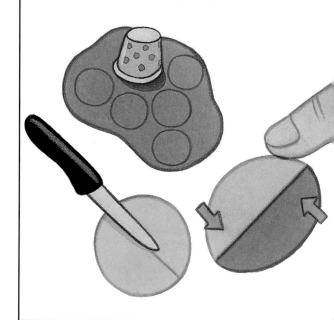

3 With the blue clay at the top of the oval and the purple at the bottom, use the knife to draw lines from the top of each oval to the bottom. Flip the ovals over and draw lines on the other side also.

4 To make a petal, gather an oval by folding the purple clay like a fan, as shown. Repeat with all the ovals.

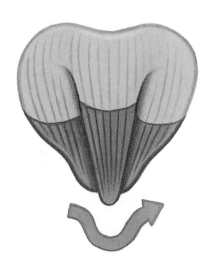

5 Put two petals together and press the bottom edges together to make the centre of one flower. Arrange four petals, overlapping each other, around the centre. Press all of them together firmly at the base and cut the base off to make it flat. Repeat for the second earring.

6 Place the camellias on the baking tray and bake them according to the directions on the packages of clay. When the camellias are cool, glue an earring post or clip to the back of each one.

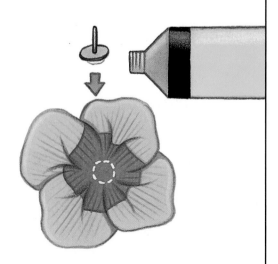

Rainforest parrot earrings

YOU WILL NEED

CLAY

parrot green (*one small marble-size piece*)

periwinkle blue (*one small marble-size piece*)

light green (*two small marble-size pieces*)

light tangerine (*one small marble-size piece*)

tangerine (*one small marble-size piece*)

parrot blue (*one small marble-size piece*)

sun yellow (*two dots*)

#9 black (*two dots*)

---

two 7-mm earring posts and ear clutches
or two 15-mm earring clips

kitchen knife, baking tray,

two-part epoxy glue

1 Set aside one ball of light green clay, and all the yellow clay and the black clay. Roll each of the remaining pieces of clay into logs 0.5 cm (¼ in.) in diameter.

2 Arrange the logs as shown. The parrot green will be the head and the parrot blue will be the tail.

3 Cut two rectangles out of the clay logs, each one measuring 1 cm x 4 cm (⅜ in. x 1½ in.). Shape each rectangle into a ball by pressing the logs together gently.

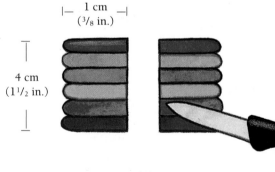

4 Take one ball and, with the parrot green at the top and the parrot blue at the bottom, flatten the ball between your thumb and forefinger. Try to keep all six colours visible.

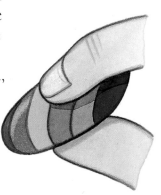

5 To make the head, gently squeeze and curve the parrot green part of the ball as shown. To form the tail, squeeze the blue together. Repeat with the second ball, but shape the second parrot so it faces in the opposite direction to the first parrot.

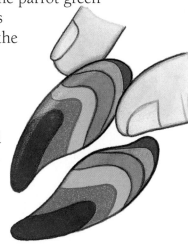

6 To make the beaks, roll the remaining piece of light green clay into a log 0.5 cm (¼ in.) in diameter. Cut two thin discs, flatten them slightly, smooth the edges, and press them onto the heads. Cut into each circle one-third of the way to make a slit resembling an open beak.

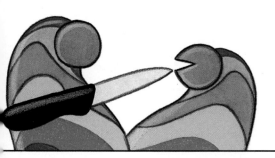

7 To make the wings, cut two 1-cm (³⁄₈-in.) long pieces from the light green log. Form each piece into a teardrop shape. With the knife, draw lines that meet at the tip of each wing. Place a wing on each parrot, as shown.

8 To finish the tail, roll a thin, even line of light green clay. Cut two lines, each 1.5 cm (⅝ in.) long, and two lines 2 cm (¾ in.) long. Place a longer line on the inside of each tail and a shorter line on the outside. Press the lines down gently.

9 To make the eyes, press a yellow dot onto each face for an eye base. Press a smaller black dot onto each yellow dot.

10 Place the parrots on the baking tray and bake them according to the directions on the packages of clay. When the parrots are cool, glue an earring post to the back of the head of each one.

Chapter Four

PETAL DISCING

Pins, earrings, shoe-clips — once you learn how to make flower petals from discs of clay, you can make many beautiful flowers and pieces of jewellery.

Calla lily earrings

YOU WILL NEED

CLAY
dark pink (*two pea-size pieces*)
medium pink (*two pea-size pieces*)
light pink (*two pea-size pieces*)
light green (*four pea-size pieces*)

---

two 7-mm earring posts and ear clutches
or two 15-mm earring clips
kitchen knife, baking tray,
two-part epoxy glue

1 To make the petals, flatten each of the pink balls of clay into smooth round discs. Each of the six discs should measure about 2 cm (¾ in.) in diameter, or about the size of a nickel.

2 To shape each petal, curl one side of a disc towards the centre, then curl the other side over the first side. Repeat with all discs.

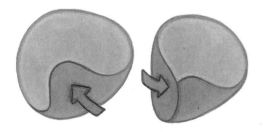

3 To make the leaves, flatten each ball of green clay and shape it into a rounded diamond. The finished leaves should each measure about 2 cm x 1 cm (¾ in. x ⅜ in.). Draw lines on the leaves with the knife, as shown. Gently bend the leaves inward along the centre line.

4 To make a flower, take one each of the light, medium and dark pink curled petals and press them gently together at their bases with the curled side facing towards the centre. Repeat with the other three petals to make the other flower.

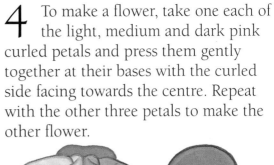

5 Add two leaves between any two petals and press them to the base of the flower. Cut the bases off the flowers to make them flat.

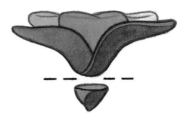

6 Place the calla lilies on the baking tray and bake them according to the directions on the packages of clay. When the lilies are cool, glue an earring post or clip to the base of each one.

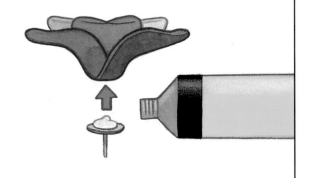

Wisteria barrette

YOU WILL NEED

CLAY

turquoise green
*(one large marble-size and
two pea-size pieces)*

light purple *(four pea-size pieces)*

medium purple *(four pea-size pieces)*

dark purple *(four pea-size pieces)*

4-mm knitting needle

French barrette, 7 cm (2 ¾ in.) long

kitchen knife, baking tray,

two-part epoxy glue

1 To make the leaf base, shape the marble-size piece of green clay into a long, pointed leaf about 9 cm x 1.5 cm (3 ½ in. x ⅝ in.) and 0.3 cm (⅛ in.) thick. With the knife, draw lines on it, as shown.

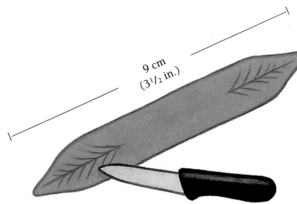

9 cm
(3½ in.)

2 To make the petals, take each purple ball of clay and flatten it into a smooth, flat oval. Each oval should be 3 cm x 1.5 cm (1⅛ in. x ⅝ in.). To make the discs into petals, fold each one about three times like a fan, as shown.

3 To make a flower, take four of the same colour petals and press their bases together. Cut the base off to make it flat. Repeat with the other two purple colours to make the other flowers.

5 To make the leaves for either end of the barrette, flatten each pea-sized piece of green clay and shape each one into a rounded diamond. With the knife, draw lines on each leaf, as shown. Bend each leaf inward along the centre line and pinch one end. Attach a leaf at each end of the barrette.

4 To assemble the wisteria, take the dark purple flower and place it on the leaf about 2.5 cm (1 in.) from one end. Secure it to the leaf by pressing down between the ruffles with the tip of the knitting needle. Place the medium purple flower on the leaf, close to the first flower, and attach it the same way. Repeat for the light purple flower.

6 Lay the wisteria on the barrette so that it will take the curved shape of the barrette as they bake together.

7 Place the wisteria barrette on the baking tray and bake it according to the directions on the packages of clay. When the wisteria is cool, glue it to the barrette.

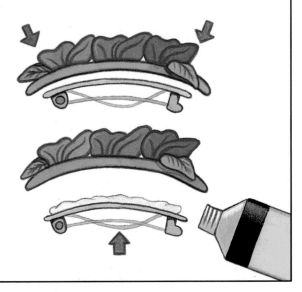

Rose shoe-clips

1 To make the petals, press ten of the balls of red clay into smooth, even discs. Six of the discs should measure 2.5 cm (1 in.) in diameter, or about the size of a quarter and four of the discs should measure 2 cm (¾ in.) in diameter, or about the size of a nickel.

2 Place a disc in the palm of your hand and press down the middle with your forefinger to give the disc a bowl shape. Then pinch one side of the disc together to make a stem. While you are holding the stem in one hand, use your other thumb and forefinger to curl back both sides of the petal disc to make a soft point at the top, as shown. Repeat for all the discs.

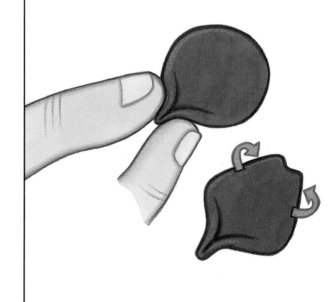

YOU WILL NEED

CLAY

#29 carmine (red)
(*eleven pea-size pieces*)

emerald green (*four pea-size pieces*)

4-mm knitting needle

two shoe-clips

kitchen knife, baking tray,

two-part epoxy glue

3 To make the centre buds, cut the remaining ball of red clay in half. Roll each half into a ball, then round one side of each ball into a point and pinch the opposite side to make a stem.

4 To make a rose, put two of the smaller petals on opposite sides of a centre bud. Place three of the larger petals evenly around the base of those petals. Press them gently together at the base. Repeat for the other rose.

5 To make the leaves, shape each ball of green clay into a rounded diamond. The finished leaves should each measure about 2 cm x 1.5 cm (¾ in. x ⅝ in.). Draw veins on the leaves with the knife, as shown. Bend the leaves gently inward along the centre line.

6 Add two leaves to each rose by placing the leaves between any two of the outer petals. Cut the base off each flower so that it is flat.

7 Place the roses on the baking tray and bake them according to the directions on the packages of clay. When the roses are cool, glue a shoe clip to the base of each one.

Ruffled bouquet pin

YOU WILL NEED

CLAY

parrot blue *(one large marble-size piece)*

periwinkle blue *(one large marble-size piece)*

medium purple *(one large marble-size piece)*

turquoise green *(one large marble-size piece)*

4-mm knitting needle

brooch pin

kitchen knife, baking tray,

two-part epoxy glue

1 Flatten the parrot blue clay, periwinkle blue clay and medium purple clay into thin strips, each about 1.5 cm (⅝ in.) wide and 15 cm (6 in.) long.

2 To make each ruffled flower, gather each strip by folding it back and forth like a fan and pinching the bottom gently as you work. Each fold should be about 0.5 cm (¼ in.) wide. Curl the ruffled strip into a flower, as shown. To make the bouquet, press the bases of the flowers together.

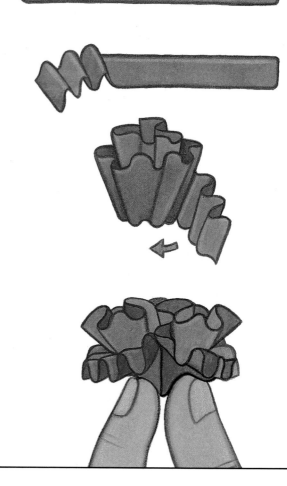

15 cm
(6 in.)

3 To make the leaves, roll the green clay into a log about 3 cm (1 ⅛ in.) long and cut it into three equal pieces. Flatten each piece of clay, then pinch two sides to form points. Draw veins on the leaves with the knife, as shown. Gently bend the leaves in along the centre line.

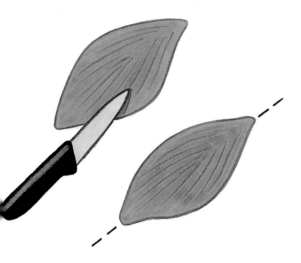

4 Attach each of the three leaves to the base, where the flowers are joined together. Cut the base off the bouquet to make it flat.

5 Place the bouquet on the baking tray and bake it according to the directions on the packages of clay. When the bouquet is cool, glue the brooch pin to its base.

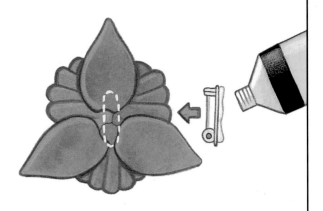

OTHER IDEAS

Make earrings to match your pin. Flatten two pea-size pieces of medium purple clay into strips, each 1 cm (⅜ in.) wide and 4.5 cm (1¾ in.) long. Gather each strip and fold it like a fan, pinching the bottom gently as you work. Curl the ruffled strip into a flower. To make the leaves, cut a small marble-size piece of turquoise green clay into four pieces and shape the clay as described in step 3. Attach two leaves to the base of each flower and cut the base flat. Bake and, when cool, glue on earring posts.

Chapter Five

HAND-BUILDING

You won't need stencils or cookie cutters for the jewellery in this chapter. You can make beautiful earrings, pins, rings and necklaces just using your hands.

Starfish and shell earrings

YOU WILL NEED

CLAY
medium purple
(one small marble-size piece)
turquoise blue
(one small marble-size piece)

---

seashell

two 7-mm earring posts and ear clutches
or two 15-mm earring clips

kitchen knife, baking tray,

two-part epoxy glue

1 To make the shell, flatten the purple clay and form it into a fat teardrop shape. Press the clay onto the shell and press down on it until it picks up the shell's texture. Carefully peel the clay off the shell. If the clay sticks, remove it from the shell, put a little cooking oil on the shell and try again.

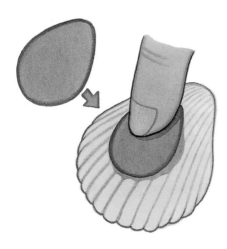

3 To make the starfish, roll the blue clay into a ball and flatten it until you have a disc about 2 cm (¾ in.) in diameter. With the knife, cut five wedges from the disc, as shown. Shape and smooth the edges of the star.

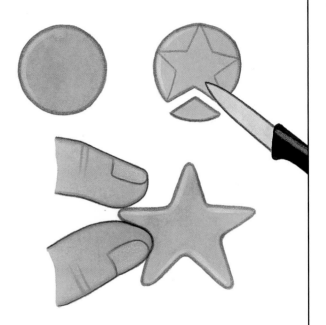

2 To make the barnacle, place a dot of blue clay on the lower portion of the shell. Press it in place with the tip of the knife to give it texture.

4 Place the pieces on the baking tray and bake them according to the directions on the packages of clay. When the pieces are cool, glue an earring post or clip to the back of each one.

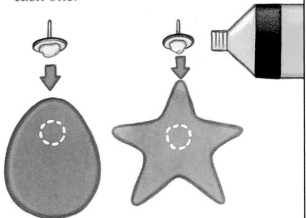

Ladybug ring

1 To make the body, press one ball of red clay into a fat oval about 2 cm (¾ in.) long, 1.5 cm (⅝ in.) wide and 1 cm (⅜ in.) thick.

2 Cut the black clay in half. To make the head, press one of the halves into a flat oval. Lay it on the top of one end of the body. Press it down all the way around to make it smooth.

3 To decorate the body, roll the remaining black clay into a thin line. Place the line down the centre of the back and cut off the extra. To make the dots, cut ten dots from the remaining black clay. Press them onto the body.

4 To make the eyes, place two white dots on the head.

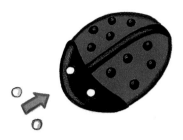

5 To make the ring loop, roll the remaining red clay into a log 0.3 cm (⅛ in.) in diameter. Wrap it around the finger that you want the ring to fit. Cut the log 0.5 cm (¼ in.) longer than the size of your finger. Make a circle by overlapping the ends of the log. Press the joined ends of the ring gently to make a flat base for gluing on the ladybug.

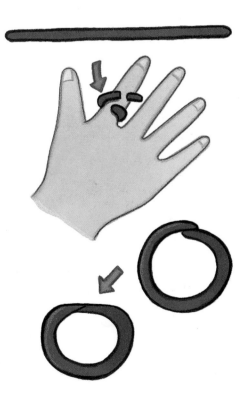

6 Place the pieces on the baking tray and bake them according to the directions on the packages of clay. When the pieces are cool, glue the ladybug to the ring.

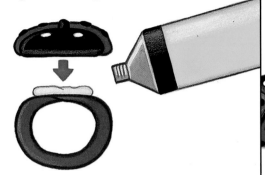

OTHER IDEAS

Ladybugs also make great earrings, pins, button covers and necklaces. For earrings, make two ladybugs following steps 1 to 4. Bake your clay, then when it's cool, glue a 7-mm earring post or 15-mm clip to the back of each ladybug. To make pins or button covers, follow steps 1 to 4 and 6, then glue a small brooch pin or button cover to the back of each ladybug. You can also add a loop to the back of a larger ladybug and string it along with beads to make a necklace (see page 7).

Cherry earrings

1 To make the cherries, use the four balls of red clay. Flatten each one but keep the centres thicker than the edges. To make each cherry rounded, place it in the palm of your hand and press the centre down with your forefinger to make a slight bowl shape.

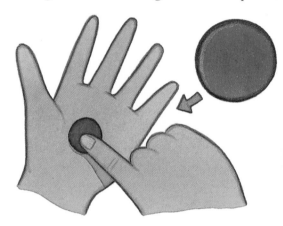

2 To make the stems, roll each piece of bronze clay into a thick line 7 cm (2 3/4 in.) long. Fold each line into an upside-down **V** and gently pinch the centre of the **V**.

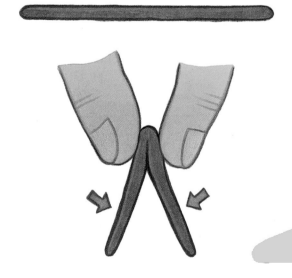

3 To make an earring, place one cherry, rounded side up, on a left-hand stem, overlapping the bottom of it by about 1 cm (³⁄₈ in.). Overlap the second cherry on the first cherry and the other stem and press down gently. Repeat for the second earring, this time overlapping the left cherry over the right.

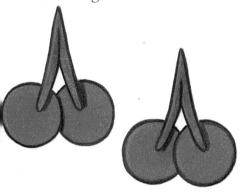

4 To make the leaves, cut each ball of green clay in half and roll each piece into a ball. Flatten each ball and shape it into a rounded diamond. With the knife, draw lines on the leaves.

5 Bend each leaf inward along the centre line and pinch one end of each leaf. To make four sets of leaves, attach each emerald green leaf beside a light green leaf at the pinched ends.

6 Place one set of leaves over the fold in the stem so that the pinched ends sit on top of the stem and the tips of the leaves rest on the cherries. Press down gently. With the needle, make a hole for the jump rings at the top of the stem. Repeat for the second earring.

7 To make the leaf pads, use the needle to make holes across the bases of the remaining two sets of joined leaves.

8 Place the pieces on the baking tray and bake them according to the directions on the packages of clay. When the pieces are cool, use the pliers to attach the jump rings and join each cherry to a leaf pad. Glue an earring post or clip to the back of each leaf pad.

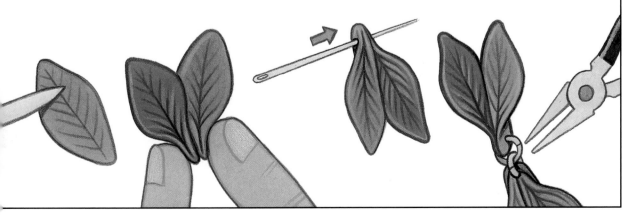

Clown pin

YOU WILL NEED

CLAY

#29 carmine (red) *(three pea-size pieces)*

turquoise green
(four pea-size pieces)

#37 blue *(one small marble-size piece
and two dots)*

sun yellow *(two pea-size pieces)*

dark pink
(three pea-size pieces and two dots)

medium purple *(one pea-size piece)*

#28 apricot *(one small marble-size piece)*

---

brooch pin

kitchen knife, baking tray,

two-part epoxy glue

1 To make the pants, roll a pea-size piece of the red, blue, yellow and green clay into logs, each 1.5 cm (⁵⁄₈ in.) long. Attach the red piece of clay to the blue by pressing the two pieces together to make one pant leg. Then press the yellow to the green to make the other. Shape each pant leg into a smooth, flat oval. Try to make each colour show an equal amount on each leg. Lay one pant leg beside the other, overlapping them at the crotch. With the knife, draw vertical lines on the pants.

1.5 cm
(⁵⁄₈ in.)

2 To make the sleeves, use a pea-sized piece of both the red and the green clay. Flatten both pieces into bell shapes. Join the narrower ends to the top of the legs, as shown.

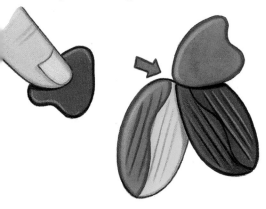

3 To make the collar, cut the ball of purple clay into five equal pieces. Shape each piece into a long oval with pointed ends. Lay one oval over another around the top of the sleeves, as shown. Cut five dots from a ball of the green clay for pompoms and press them on the tips of the collar.

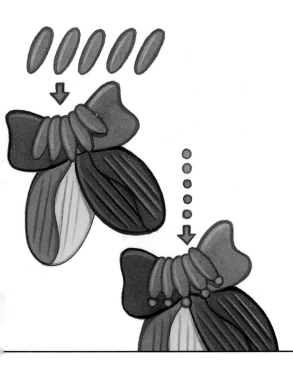

4 To make the head, roll the flesh-coloured clay into a log about 2.5 cm (1 in.) long. Cut a piece 0.5 cm (¼ in.) long off the log. Roll the piece into a ball and press it into an oval. Position the oval so that it slightly overlaps the collar and press it gently in place. Put the two dots of blue clay halfway down the face for eyes. Put a dot of red clay under the eyes for the nose. For the mouth, roll a small ball of red clay into a thin line, curve it and place it under the nose. Put a dot of pink clay on each end of the mouth for the cheeks.

5 To make the hands, cut two pieces 0.3 cm (⅛ in.) long off the flesh-coloured log. Shape each piece as shown. Make a slit down one-third of each oval to separate the thumb from the fingers and smooth out the edges. Place one hand under each sleeve.

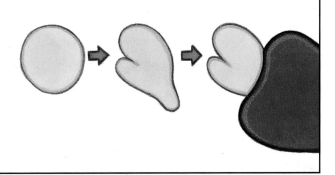

6 To make the shoes, flatten and shape two balls of the pink clay into shoes as shown. Place one under each pant leg and press down gently. Roll two yellow dots for the pompoms.

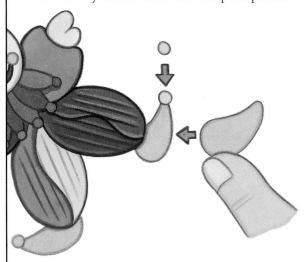

7 To make the pink ruffle for the hat, flatten a ball of pink clay into a rectangle about 5 cm x 1 cm (2 in. x ⅜ in.). Fold the rectangle like a fan as shown. Press the ruffle down gently at the top of the head.

8 To make the hat, flatten and form a ball of green clay into a fat teardrop shape and lay it over the pink ruffle. Roll a yellow dot for a pompom and place it on the tip of the hat.

OTHER IDEAS

Try making a clown necklace. See pages 6 and 7 for instructions on how to add a loop to the back of the clown's head and hat, how to make beads and a cord top (use the same colours of clay you used for the clown), and how to string your necklace. Turquoise satin cord looks great with these colours of clay.